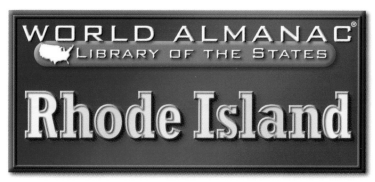

Rhode Island

THE OCEAN STATE

by Joanne Mattern

WORLD ALMANAC® LIBRARY

Please visit our web site at: **www.worldalmanaclibrary.com**
**For a free color catalog describing World Almanac® Library's list of high-quality books
and multimedia programs, call 1-800-848-2928 (USA) or 1-800-387-3178 (Canada).
World Almanac® Library's fax: (414) 332-3567.**

Library of Congress Cataloging-in-Publication Data

Mattern, Joanne, 1963-
    Rhode Island, the Ocean State / by Joanne Mattern.
      p. cm. — (World Almanac Library of the states)
    Includes bibliographical references and index.
    Summary: Presents the history, geography, people, government, economy,
social life and customs, and state events and attractions of Rhode Island.
    ISBN 0-8368-5159-5 (lib. bdg.)
    ISBN 0-8368-5330-X (softcover)
    1. Rhode Island—Juvenile literature. [1. Rhode Island.] I. Title. II. Series.
F79.3.M36   2003
974.5—dc21   2002043106

First published in 2003 by
World Almanac® Library
330 West Olive Street, Suite 100
Milwaukee, WI 53212 USA

Copyright © 2003 by World Almanac® Library.

A Creative Media Applications Production
Design: Alan Barnett, Inc.
Copy editor: Laurie Lieb
Fact checker: Joan Vernero
Photo researcher: Annette Cyr
World Almanac® Library project editor: Tim Paulson
World Almanac® Library editors: Mary Dykstra, Gustav Gedatus, Jacqueline Laks Gorman,
  Lyman Lyons
World Almanac® Library art direction: Tammy Gruenewald
World Almanac® Library graphic designers: Scott M. Krall, Melissa Valuch

Photo credits: pp. 4-5 © Rhode Island Division of Tourism; p. 6 (left) © Rhode Island Division of
Tourism; p. 6 (right bottom) © North Wind Picture Archives; p. 6 (right top) © Rhode Island
Division of Tourism; p. 7 (top) © AP Photo/Stew Milne; p. 7 (bottom) © Hulton Archives/Getty
Images; p. 9 © Rhode Island Division of Tourism; p. 10 © Hulton Archives/Getty Images; p. 11
© North Wind Picture Archives; p. 12 © North Wind Picture Archives; p. 13 © North Wind
Picture Archives; p. 14 © North Wind Picture Archives; p. 15 © Bob Rowan, Progressive
Image/Corbis; p. 17 © AP Photo/Joe Giblin; p. 18 © Rhode Island Division of Tourism; p. 19
© Hulton Archives/Getty Images; p. 20 (left) © Rhode Island Division of Tourism; p. 20 (center)
© ArtToday; p. 20 (right) © AP Photo/Victoria Arocho; p. 21 (left) © AP/Wide World Photos; p. 21
(center) © Rhode Island Division of Tourism; p. 21 (right) © Rhode Island Division of Tourism;
p. 23 © AP Photo/Victoria Arocho; p. 26 © Rhode Island Division of Tourism; p. 27 © AP
Photo/Paul Connors; p. 29 © Rhode Island Division of Tourism; p. 31 (top) © AP Photo/Matt York;
p. 31 (bottom) © AP Photo/Matt York; p. 32 © Hulton Archives/Getty Images; p. 33 © AP
Photo/Newport Daily News; p. 34 © AP Photo/Matt York; p. 35 © AP Photo/Matt York; p. 36
© Rhode Island Division of Tourism; p. 37 (top) © National Baseball Hall of Fame and Museum;
p. 37 (bottom) © National Baseball Hall of Fame and Museum; p. 38 © North Wind Picture
Archives; p. 39 (left) © Hulton Archives/Getty Images; p. 39 (right) © Hulton Archives/Getty
Images; p. 40 © North Wind Picture Archives; p. 41 © Hulton Archives/Getty Images; pp. 42-43
© North Wind Picture Archives; p. 44 (top) © AP Photo/Jon-Pierre Lasseigne; p. 44 (bottom)
© Photodisc/Getty Images; p. 45 (top) © AP Photo/Gail Oskin; p. 45 (bottom) © Catherine
Karnow/Corbis

Printed in the United States of America

1 2 3 4 5 6 7 8 9 07 06 05 04 03

Rhode Island

The Smallest State

Geographically, Rhode Island is the smallest state in the nation. But there is nothing else that is small about this New England state! Rhode Island is a treasure chest filled with natural wonders, rich history, and a diverse, vibrant population. The state's long coastline, sandy beaches, islands, and mild ocean climate make it a popular vacation destination for thousands of residents and visitors each year.

Rhode Island's history as an American colony dates back to 1636, when Roger Williams established a settlement where people could worship as they chose. As the colony grew, it welcomed those who were not welcomed elsewhere.

During the Revolutionary War, Rhode Islanders played a key role in shaping their new nation, the United States of America. One of the thirteen original colonies, Rhode Island was the first colony to declare and fight for freedom from Great Britain. Fiercely proud of its newly gained independence, the state was the last of the thirteen original colonies to ratify the U.S. Constitution in 1790.

In the late 1700s, Rhode Island was the birthplace of the American Industrial Revolution. Textile and other types of factories attracted immigrants from around the world. People from Ireland, Portugal, Italy, Canada, and other nations helped make the state a culturally rich place to live. Today, new groups of immigrants continue to come to Rhode Island in search of a better way of life.

As manufacturing declined in the state, Rhode Island's economy suffered. Today, however, commerce and industry are thriving in Rhode Island. The state's greatest asset is its people. Rhode Islanders take pride in their state's history of strength, hope, diversity, and change. The future looks bright for the smallest U.S. state.

▶ Map of Rhode Island showing the interstate highway system, as well as major cities and waterways.

▼ Southeast Lighthouse on Block Island has guarded the Atlantic sea lanes since 1874. In 1993, the 2,000-ton (1,814 metric ton) structure was moved 360 feet (110 meters) to prevent it from falling into the ocean due to the eroding cliffs on which it was perched.

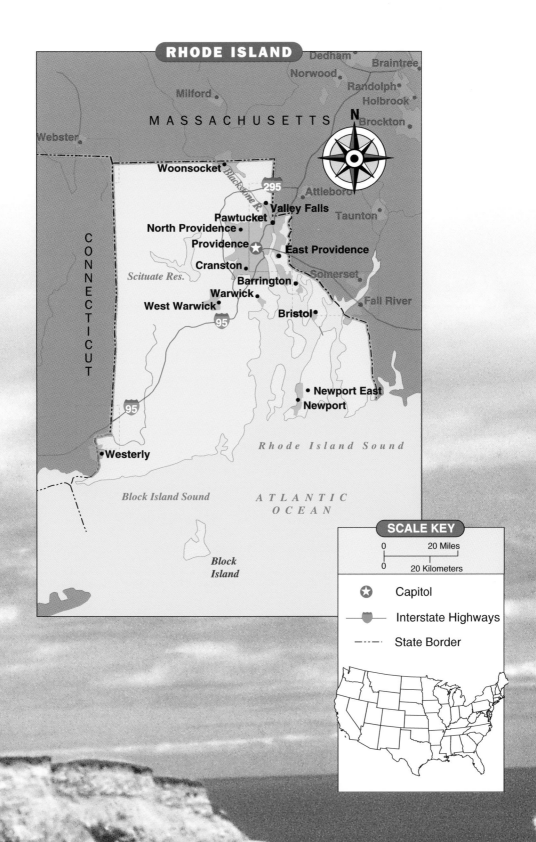

RHODE ISLAND

Dedham
Braintree
Norwood
Randolph
Milford
Holbrook
Brockton

M A S S A C H U S E T T S

Webster

N

Woonsocket
Blackstone R.
295
Attleboro
Valley Falls
Taunton
Pawtucket
North Providence
Providence
East Providence
Somerset
Cranston
Scituate Res.
Barrington
Fall River
Warwick
West Warwick
Bristol
95

C O N N E C T I C U T

Newport East
Newport

Rhode Island Sound

Westerly

Block Island Sound
A T L A N T I C
O C E A N

*Block
Island*

SCALE KEY

0   20 Miles

0   20 Kilometers

⭐ Capitol

Interstate Highways

–··– State Border

Fast Facts

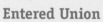

RHODE ISLAND (RI), The Ocean State, Little Rhody, The Plantation State

Entered Union

May 29, 1790 (13th state)

Capital	Population
Providence	173,618

Total Population (2000)

1,048,319 (43rd most populous state) — *Between 1990 and 2000, the state's population increased 4.5 percent.*

Largest Cities	Population
Providence	173,618
Warwick	85,808
Cranston	79,269
Pawtucket	72,958
East Providence	48,688

Land Area

1,045 square miles (2,707 square kilometers) (50th largest state)

State Motto

"Hope"

State Song

"Rhode Island's It for Me," *lyrics by Charlie Hall, music by Maria Day, adopted in 1996.*

State Bird

Rhode Island Red

State Fish

Striped bass

State Flower

Violet

State Tree

Red maple

State Fruit

Rhode Island greening — *This apple, developed in Rhode Island around 1796, has a sharp taste and a yellow-green color.*

State Shell

Quahog

State Rock

Cumberlandite — *This magnetic rock, black or dark brown in color, is found only in Rhode Island.*

State Mineral

Bowenite — *A semiprecious stone, bowenite is a relative of jade. It comes in yellow, green, gray, and blue.*

State Symbol of American Folk Art

Charles I. D. Looff Carousel — *Built in 1895 in East Providence, it is also known as the Crescent Park carousel.*

State Flagship

Providence — *This tall ship is a replica of a Revolutionary War sailing vessel.*

State Drink

Coffee milk

PLACES TO VISIT

Cliff Walk, *Newport*
This 3.5-mile (5.6 kilometer) National Recreation Trail follows Newport's southeastern shoreline. Along the walkway, visitors can see the town's famous mansions.

Roger Williams National Memorial, *Providence*
A beautiful 4.5-acre (1.8 hectare) park commemorates the founding of Providence in 1636 by Roger Williams.

Slater Mill Historic Site, *Pawtucket*
The first water-powered cotton mill in the United States is now a museum housing tools, machinery, textiles, and other artifacts that tell the story of the birth of the Industrial Revolution in New England.

For other places and events, see p. 44.

BIGGEST, BEST, AND MOST

- The biggest bug in the world is located on the roof of New England Pest Control in Providence. The metal model of a termite measures 58 feet (17.7 m) long and is 928 times the size of a real termite.

- The longest-running continuous Fourth of July celebrations have been taking place in Bristol every summer since 1785.

- Rhode Island is the smallest state in the nation — but it has the longest name. Its official state name is the State of Rhode Island and Providence Plantations.

STATE FIRSTS

- 1763 Touro Synagogue, the first in the United States, was dedicated in Newport.

- 1774 The circus made its U.S. debut in Newport.

- 1778 The first African-American army unit was formed in Rhode Island. Slaves were offered their freedom if they enlisted in the Black Regiment.

- 1953 Ann & Hope, the country's first discount department store, opened in Cumberland.

Mr. Potato Head

In 1952, one of Rhode Island's most famous residents was born: Mr. Potato Head. This superspud was invented by the Hasbro toy company in Pawtucket. In 2000, Mr. Potato Head was named Rhode Island's official tourism ambassador. Forty-seven giant Mr. and Mrs. Potato Head statues were hidden throughout the state. Thousands of visitors took part in the "spud search."

An American Eating Tradition

One morning in 1872, Walter Scott filled a horse-drawn delivery van with sandwiches and coffee. Then he and his horse wandered from factory to factory in Providence. Scott's customers ordered cheese sandwiches, boiled eggs, drinks, slices of pie, and other foods through two windows cut into the wagon's sides. Scott's idea was a hit, and more "lunch wagons" began popping up in Providence and other nearby cities. Some lunch wagons stayed open all night long to serve late-night workers. Others had spaces inside the wagon where customers could stand and eat. Eventually, some food vendors decided to keep their lunch wagons in one place all the time. This new type of restaurant became an American eating tradition: the diner.

Hope and Independence

> To hold forth a lively experiment that a most flourishing
> civil state may stand and best be maintained with
> full liberty in religious concernments.
>
> — *from Rhode Island's Royal Charter of 1663*

More than eight thousand years ago, Paleo-Indians, the first people to settle in North America, had arrived in the area that is now Rhode Island. These Paleo-Indians were the ancestors of later Native Americans who lived throughout the region. They began as small groups of nomadic hunter-gatherers, but later groups settled in villages and planted crops of corn, pumpkins, squashes, and beans. People living by the ocean fished and gathered mussels and clams.

When Europeans first settled in the region in the early 1600s, there were five main Native American groups in Rhode Island: the Narragansett, Niantic, Nipmuc, Pequot, and Wampanoag. The largest, most powerful group was the Narragansett. The Narragansett had eight major villages, each with its own leader. The chief of the largest village, located near what is now Kingston, ruled over the rest of the chiefs. In 1674, there were about five thousand Narragansett living in the area.

Native Americans of Rhode Island

Narragansett

Niantic

Nipmuc

Pequot

Sakonnet

Wampanoag

Westo

European Exploration and Settlement

The first European to explore the Rhode Island coastline may have been Portuguese explorer Miguel Corte-Real in the early 1500s. The first documented European landing in the area occurred in 1524, when the Italian adventurer Giovanni da Verrazano sailed into what is now called Narragansett Bay. In the early 1600s, Dutch traders explored the region. In 1614, Adriaen Block discovered the island off Rhode Island's coast that bears his name.

In 1636, a preacher named Roger Williams was banished from the Massachusetts Bay Colony for his religious and political beliefs. Williams received permission from the

DID YOU KNOW?

The origin of the name "Rhode Island" is disputed. Some people believe that the state was named by Giovanni da Verrazano for Rhodes, a Mediterranean island. Others believe it was called *Roodt Eylandt,* or "red island," by Dutch explorers.

Narragansett people to establish a settlement along the Seekonk River. He and his fellow settlers named the first permanent white settlement in the region "Providence." Today, Williams's settlement is the state's capital and largest city.

Soon, other people seeking the freedom to worship as they pleased began migrating from Massachusetts to the area. In 1638, Anne Hutchinson founded Portsmouth. Hutchinson was a member of a religious group that Protestant officials in Massachusetts had dubbed the Antinomians, from the Latin and Greek words for "against the law." Like Williams, Hutchinson had been banished from the Massachusetts Bay Colony for her radical religious beliefs. The following year, William Coddington, a former follower of Hutchinson's, settled Newport, and Rhode Island's fourth settlement, Warwick, was founded in 1642. All four original towns were founded as havens for people who were being persecuted for their religious beliefs. Other religious groups that settled in Rhode Island to escape persecution included Baptists, Quakers, and Jews.

In the 1630s and 1640s, Massachusetts Bay Colony officials tried to claim that the four Rhode Island

▼ Arriving in Rhode Island, Roger Williams is greeted by members of the Narragansett.

settlements were under their control. To settle the matter, Roger Williams traveled to Great Britain in 1643. The following year, he obtained a charter from the British king that united Providence, Portsmouth, Newport, and Warwick as a single colony called the Providence Plantations. In 1663, Great Britain's king granted another charter, under the name Rhode Island and the Providence Plantations, guaranteeing the colony religious freedom and self-government. This document remained in effect until 1843.

Relations between the European settlers and the Native Americans remained friendly until King Philip's War in 1675, when a Wampanoag leader named Metacom or Metacomet (called King Philip by the settlers) united Native people in the region. Metacom hoped to regain land in Massachusetts that the settlers had taken. The Indians attacked isolated settlements, destroying towns and killing colonists. At first, Rhode Island's Narragansett stayed out of the bloody struggle. However, in December 1675, colonists from Massachusetts attacked a Narragansett winter camp near what is now South Kingstown. At the Great Swamp Fight, hundreds of Narragansett, mostly women and children, were killed. Afterward, surviving Narragansett joined the warring Native groups. In March 1676, the Narragansett attacked and burned Providence, destroying most of the buildings there. King Philip's War ended in August 1676, when Metacom was killed. After the war, most

◄ Metacom was the son of Massasoit, the sachem — or leader — of the Wampanoag who governed most of what is now Massachusetts and Rhode Island. Massasoit became a friend and ally of the Pilgrims in Plymouth and signed the earliest known treaty between Indians and European settlers.

Native people in the region were wiped out. Many of the Native American warriors who had taken part in the fighting were executed or sold into slavery, and the Indians' lands were taken.

Breaking with the British

Rhode Island quickly grew into an important trading center. Corn, livestock, lumber, fish, and wool from the colony were shipped to Great Britain, the West Indies, and other colonies up and down the Atlantic coast. Newport and Providence rapidly grew into bustling port cities.

Most of the colony's wealth, however, came as a result of the slave trade in which some Rhode Island merchants engaged. In Rhode Island, molasses from the West Indies was made into rum, which was then shipped to Africa and used to buy slaves. African slaves were then brought to the West Indies and exchanged for more molasses as well as sugar and other goods. Newport and Bristol were both centers for this "triangular trade." Rhode Island slave ships continued bringing Africans to the Americas until 1807.

The more Rhode Island prospered, the more Great Britain desired to share in the colony's wealth. Soon, the British passed trade restrictions and placed heavy taxes on goods that came to the colonies from any country but Britain. These actions angered the independent Rhode Islanders. Most Rhode Islanders were strongly supported seeking independence from Great Britain.

To keep a firm grip on its colonies, Great Britain sent more ships and troops. In March 1772, the British ship *Gaspee* arrived off the coast of Rhode Island. Its mission was to prevent colonial smuggling and make sure the colonists obeyed the Stamp Act, which placed a tax on newspapers and other printed materials. Over the next three months, the captain and crew of the *Gaspee* harassed colonial ships leaving Newport. On June 9, 1772, a colonial trading ship, the *Hannah,* refused to stop for the *Gaspee*. The captain of the *Gaspee* chased after the colonial

Roger Williams

Throughout his life, Puritan leader Roger Williams held fast to the ideal that all people should have the right to think and worship as they pleased. Born in London, England, around 1603, the young man began his career as a minister for the Church of England. By 1631, Williams had left the church, become a Puritan, and set sail for the Massachusetts Bay Colony. Once there, Williams soon upset colonial officials by refusing to recognize their authority in religious matters. He further angered them by preaching that the Native people of the area owned the land and that the English king had no right to give away their land. His ideas were branded as "erroneous and very dangerous," and Williams was expelled from the colony. He went on to secure his place in history by founding Providence. Throughout his life, Williams remained active in Rhode Island politics. He died in 1683.

vessel, but his ship soon ran aground on a sandbar. When the *Hannah* arrived in Providence, her captain told local merchants about the *Gaspee* being grounded. The city's patriots saw a chance to strike a blow for freedom. That night, a group of them rowed out to the *Gaspee,* captured its captain and crew, and set the ship on fire. The burning of the *Gaspee* was the first colonial act of rebellion against Great Britain. From that moment on, Rhode Islanders would play an important role in the struggle for freedom.

In 1775, Rhode Island sent one thousand militiamen to aid Massachusetts in its struggle against British troops. The same year, the colony organized a navy to battle British ships blockading Newport's harbor. Then, on May 4, 1776, Rhode Island became the first colony to declare its independence from Great Britain. In their declaration of freedom, Rhode Island lawmakers charged King George III with forgetting his dignity and departing from the duties and character of a good king. Two famous Rhode Island patriots were Nathanael Greene and Esek Hopkins. Greene served as second-in-

▼ Rhode Island patriots burn the British ship *Gaspee* in Providence Harbor.

command to George Washington, while Hopkins was the Continental Navy's first commander in chief.

During the war, British troops occupied Newport for nearly three years. They burned hundreds of homes, forcing thousands of residents to flee. Rhode Islanders kept fighting, and in 1779, British troops left Rhode Island for the last time. After the war, Newport recovered slowly, and Providence became the center of commerce. On May 29, 1790, Rhode Island, always wary of its independence, was the last of the original thirteen colonies to ratify the U.S. Constitution.

Revolution, Rebellion, and War

The year 1790 was momentous for Rhode Island for another reason as well: The Industrial Revolution got its start when Moses Brown and Samuel Slater built the first cotton mill, in Pawtucket near the Blackstone River. By the late 1820s, cotton processing had become the backbone of the state's economy. Later, gold plating, silverware production, and rubber manufacturing became important Rhode Island industries. Many of these new industries were located in Providence, and the city grew rapidly.

In 1842, Rhode Island residents once again showed their independent spirit. That year, Providence lawyer Thomas Wilson Dorr led a rebellion to replace the 1663 charter with a new, more liberal "People's Constitution." Under the old charter, only Rhode Island landowners had the right to vote. After trying to capture the state's arsenal, many of Dorr's supporters were arrested, and Dorr himself had to flee Rhode Island. However, the rebellion made lawmakers realize that the time had come for change. They replaced the old charter with a new constitution, ratified in 1843, that gave more people voting rights.

In 1861, the Civil War between the North and South began. More than twenty-five thousand Rhode Islanders fought for the Union during the Civil War; 1,685 of them gave their lives to keep the United States whole. Those who remained at home did their part for the war effort, too. Factory workers churned out uniforms, coats, blankets, guns, cannons, sabers, and musket parts to aid the Northern armies. One company made engines for two Union warships. During the war, the United States Naval Academy relocated

▲ Oliver Hazard Perry was born in South Kingston in 1785. He became a national hero in the War of 1812 when he defeated an entire British squadron and captured all the enemy ships.

The Gettysburg Gun

The Gettysburg gun inside Rhode Island's State House is a reminder of a dark period in the nation's history. The cannon was last used in 1863 by the First Rhode Island Light Artillery during the Battle of Gettysburg. When the big gun was hit by an enemy shell during the fight, a cannonball got jammed in its muzzle. The cannonball can still be seen. The two men loading the gun were killed.

from Annapolis, Maryland, to Newport for four years.

For decades after the Civil War, industry thrived in Rhode Island. Manufacturing jobs attracted thousands of immigrants who came to the United States seeking a better way of life. These people journeyed from Canada, Germany, Sweden, Italy, Portugal, Greece, Ireland, and other countries in eastern and southern Europe. In the late 1800s, the so-called Gilded Age, Rhode Island attracted the rich and famous. Newport became a summer vacation center where the nation's millionaires enjoyed dinner parties, fox hunts, polo games, and other favored activities. To house themselves and their guests, the Astors, Vanderbilts, and other well-to-do families built huge mansions, which they called "summer cottages." Today, the mansions of Newport are an attraction that draws visitors from around the world. One of the palatial mansions is Rosecliff, completed in 1902. The house, built for Nevada silver heiress Theresa Fair Oelrichs, was modeled after Versailles, a famous French palace. With the largest ballroom in Newport, Rosecliff was the site of some of the town's most unusual and extravagant parties. One such party was the White Ball, held in 1904. For the event, Rosecliff was filled with white flowers, and ladies who attended wore white dresses and powdered their hair.

▲ Textile manufacturing became an important Rhode Island industry in the early 1800s. Mills such as this one on the Blackstone River in Pawtucket were among the first successful cotton mills in the United States.

Hard Times, Good Times

Manufacturing continued to sustain Rhode Island's economy until the 1920s, when cheaper labor could be found in the South. Many companies closed down or moved out of the region. Beginning in 1929, the Great Depression, a period of worldwide economic hardship, took a heavy toll on the state. Many towns fell on hard times as factories closed and thousands of employees were thrown out of work.

World War II, with a demand for manufactured goods, brought temporary relief to the state's economy. However, the war caused heartache and suffering for many Rhode Island families. More than ninety-two thousand men and women from the state served during the war, and more than

DID YOU KNOW?

The Breakers, one of Newport's most amazing mansions, was modeled after palaces in Italy. Built for Cornelius Vanderbilt in 1895, the massive dwelling contains seventy rooms, including a ballroom, two-story dining room, music room, library, and billiard room. The Breakers is now open to the public for guided tours.

twenty-one hundred lost their lives.

After the war, manufacturing in Rhode Island continued to decline, and many factories that had produced wartime materials closed their doors. Providence was particularly hard-hit. Many city dwellers packed up and moved to the suburbs in search of safer streets and better housing and education. In August 1954, Providence received another serious blow when Hurricane Carol hit the state, causing more than $90 million in damages statewide. A year later, Hurricane Diane caused about $170 million in damages throughout the state. The 1980s brought more problems as Rhode Islanders suffered through a series of political scandals involving top state officials and corporations.

Today, after suffering decades of tough times, Rhode Island has made a comeback. In recent years, the state has turned to other industries in addition to manufacturing for a healthy economy. Rhode Island's population continues to grow, and cities like Providence have worked hard to revitalize their downtown areas to attract visitors and residents. And constitutional reforms have ensured that Rhode Island's government functions in the most efficient, open manner possible. Rhode Islanders can look forward to a twenty-first century filled with promise.

A Serious Storm

Rhode Island has suffered its share of wicked weather. In the 1950s, two hurricanes caused serious damage across the state. Then, in early February 1978, a blizzard raged through Rhode Island. For two days, the storm dumped as much as 4 feet (1.2 m) of snow on the area. Winds of more than 60 miles (97 km) per hour toppled trees and cut off electricity to thousands of people. Travelers were forced to abandon their vehicles during the storm, leaving the highways cluttered with cars. The blizzard shut down state business for days as workers in Providence dug the city out from under the huge piles of snow. When it was all over, officials estimated that this "Storm of the Century" had cost the East Coast about $1 billion in damages.

◀ Pawtucket is home to Hasbro, Inc., one of the world's largest toy manufacturers. The company started in 1923 with eight family members working in a small shop in Providence and now employs more than ten thousand people worldwide. Shown here, workers build toys at a Hasbro factory.

Diversity and Determination

> Give to bigotry no sanction, to persecution no assistance.
>
> — *George Washington, from "A Letter to the Hebrew Congregation in Newport," 1790*

From 1990 to 2000, Rhode Island's population grew by 4.5 percent. That is well under the national average rate of 13.1 percent. In fact, Rhode Island ranked fiftieth in population growth from 1995 to 2000. Despite its low growth rate, Rhode Island has the second highest population density in the nation. With 1,003 persons per square mile (387 per sq km), Rhode Island far exceeds the national average of 80 persons per square mile (49 per sq km). Most of Rhode Island's residents (31 percent) live in urban areas.

The largest urban area is Providence, the state's capital. This city is Rhode Island's commercial, financial, and industrial center. It is also a major transportation hub: Providence Port is one of the largest seaports in New England. In recent years, new construction has added to

Age Distribution in Rhode Island
(2000 Census)

0–4	63,896
5–19	218,720
20–24	71,813
25–44	310,636
45–64	230,852
65 & over	152,402

Across One Hundred Years

Rhode Island's three largest foreign-born groups for 1890 and 1990

1890	1990
Ireland 38,920	Portugal 23,035
Canada/Newfoundland 27,934	Dominican Republic 6,408
England 20,901	Canada 6,132

Total state population: 345,506
Total foreign-born: 106,305 (30.8%)

Total state population: 1,003,464
Total foreign-born: 95,088 (9.5%)

Patterns of Immigration

The total number of people who immigrated to Rhode Island in 1998 was 1,976. Of that number, the largest immigrant groups were from the Dominican Republic (14.4%), Guatemala (7.7%), and Colombia (7.5%).

▶ Celebrators dance and make final adjustments to their costumes before the Dominican Parade which kicks off the annual Dominican Festival of Rhode Island in Providence.

the city's skyline. As Rhode Island's oldest city, Providence is also home to many historic buildings and sites.

Warwick is another urban center, and the state's second largest city. It is located on Narragansett Bay. Warwick is home to T. F. Green Airport, Rhode Island's major airport. Like Providence, Warwick combines the old and the new. Founded in 1642, the city has many historic sites. It is known as Rhode Island's retail capital for its wealth of stores and restaurants. Other major cities include Cranston, Pawtucket, and East Providence.

Ethnicities

Rhode Island is a state of great ethnic diversity. Since its earliest origins, the state has attracted people seeking better lives for themselves and their families. The first permanent settlers in Rhode Island were people from other colonies who had originally migrated to America from England. These earliest settlers were looking for religious freedom.

As a result of Rhode Island's slave trade, a significant percentage of Rhode Island's early population was African American. By the 1830s, African Americans made up 7.2

> **DID YOU KNOW?**
>
> The median age of Rhode Island's population is 36.7. By 2025, the U.S. Census has projected that Rhode Island's total population will increase by more than 92,000.

Heritage and Background, Rhode Island — Year 2000

▶ Here is a look at the racial backgrounds of Rhode Islanders today. Rhode Island ranks thirty-first among all U.S. states with regard to African Americans as a percentage of the population.

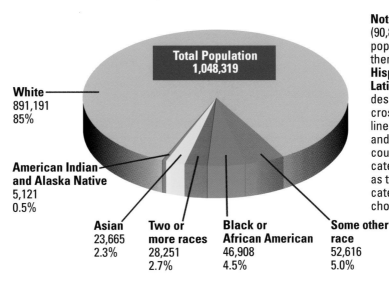

Total Population 1,048,319

White
891,191
85%

American Indian and Alaska Native
5,121
0.5%

Native Hawaiian and Other Pacific Islander
567
0.1%

Asian
23,665
2.3%

Two or more races
28,251
2.7%

Black or African American
46,908
4.5%

Some other race
52,616
5.0%

Note: 8.7% (90,820) of the population identify themselves as **Hispanic** or **Latino**, a cultural designation that crosses racial lines. Hispanics and Latinos are counted in this category as well as the racial category of their choice.

percent of Providence's population. African-American men gained the right to vote in 1842, when Rhode Island lawmakers enacted a new constitution.

During the Industrial Revolution, thousands of immigrants from other nations poured into Rhode Island. The first to arrive were Irish, French Canadian, and British. Today, 18.4 percent of all Rhode Islanders claim Irish heritage. In the late 1800s, more people came from countries in southern and eastern Europe, including Portugal, Italy, Poland, and Russia. Today, 19 percent of Rhode Island residents claim Italian ancestry.

Two ethnic groups that are growing rapidly are Hispanics and Southeast Asians. In 2000, more than half of all immigrants to Rhode Island were from these two groups.

Educational Levels of Rhode Island Residents (age 25 and over)	
Less than 9th grade	56,312
9th to 12th grade, no diploma	96,774
High school graduate, including equivalency	192,914
Some college, no degree or associate degree	170,756
Bachelor's degree	110,175
Graduate or professional degree	67,642

▼ The skyline of Providence, Rhode Island's capital and largest city.

Native Americans make up only a small percentage of the population. Most are members of the Narragansett.

Religion

Rhode Island was founded as a haven for people who wanted to worship freely. Roger Williams and other early settlers were Protestant. Williams himself founded the first Baptist church in the United States. These religious outsiders welcomed other persecuted groups. In 1658, for example, a small community of Jews settled in Newport. In 1763, the first synagogue in the United States, Touro Synagogue, was established there.

▲ Touro Synagogue in Newport, consecrated in 1763, is the oldest Jewish house of worship in the United States.

Today, more than half of all Rhode Islanders are Roman Catholic. This is the result of the massive migration of people from Catholic countries (Ireland, Portugal, Italy) that took place during the 1800s and early 1900s. Other faiths are well represented in the state, including Baptist, Church of Jesus Christ of Latter-day Saints, Episcopal, Islam, and Methodist.

Education

The first free school in Rhode Island opened in Newport in 1640. Public schooling throughout the state began in 1800, when a law was passed that required every town in the state to set up a "free school." However, many towns could not afford these schools and did not comply with the law. Finally, in 1828, Rhode Island's legislature set up a fund to help pay for public schooling. After this, the number of schools jumped in the state, from 192 in 1819 to 592 in 1831. School attendance is compulsory for Rhode Islanders aged six to sixteen. In 1999, about 14 percent of Rhode Island students attended private school.

There are several public institutes of higher learning in Rhode Island, including the University of Rhode Island and Rhode Island College. Rhode Island also has a number of excellent private colleges and universities, including Brown University, Rhode Island School of Design (RISD), Providence College, and Johnson and Wales University, all located in Providence. Other private colleges include Bryant College, Salve Regina University, and Roger Williams University.

The Naval War College

For more than a century, the Naval War College in Newport has trained officers to serve in the U.S. Navy. Established in 1884 by the U.S. secretary of the navy, the college was first lodged in the former Newport Asylum for the Poor. Since then, it has more than doubled in size and now includes the Center for Naval Warfare Studies. Here, students can take part in war games to learn battle tactics and strategies. Today, the college is the oldest continuing institution of its kind.

Small is Beautiful

> I've been to every state we have
> And I think that I'm inclined to say
> That Rhody stole my heart:
> You can keep the forty-nine.
>
> — *From "Rhode Island's It for Me," Rhode Island's state song, adopted in 1996*

Rhode Island is the smallest state in the nation. From north to south, the state measures about 47 miles (76 km). From east to west, the distance is only about 40 miles (64 km). Rhode Island's total land area is 1,045 square miles (2,707 sq km). The rectangular-shaped state is bordered on the west by Connecticut, on the north and east by Massachusetts, and on the south by the Atlantic Ocean. Rhode Island can be divided into two regions, the Coastal Lowlands and the New England Upland.

The Coastal Lowlands

The Seaboard Lowland occupies the southeastern two-thirds of Rhode Island. This area of the state is a low, sandy plain. Narragansett Bay, the state's coastline, and its coastal islands are all part of the Coastal Lowlands. Most of the state's major cities are found here.

The Coastal Lowlands region is well drained. The Pawtuxet, Seekonk, Woonasquatucket, and Blackstone

Highest Point
Jerimoth Hill 812 feet (247 m) above sea level

▼ *From left to right:* **Sailing off Newport; Napatree Point; a tall ship sails under Newport Bridge; a red fox prowls the sand dunes; the First Baptist Church, in Providence; Rhode Island seafood.**

Rivers run through the area, draining most of northern Rhode Island. The Blackstone is Rhode Island's longest river. All of these rivers empty into Narragansett Bay. The Pawcatuck River, which drains the southern section of the state, empties into the Atlantic Ocean. This river forms a section of the border between Rhode Island and Connecticut. Rhode Island's rivers contain many waterfalls.

Rhode Island's coastline measures about 40 miles (64 km) in length. Behind its long string of sandy beaches lie salt marshes, lagoons, and low hills. The coast is home to resorts, parks, and marinas that attract visitors each summer. Offshore, the largest island in Rhode Island waters is Block Island, which is about 7 miles (11 km) long and 3.5 miles (5.6 km) wide. The island is a popular summer resort area.

Narragansett Bay is the major geographical feature in Rhode Island. This inlet lies in the southeasternmost section of the state. The big bay runs north to south, measuring about 26 miles (42 km) in length and between 3 and 12 miles (5 and 19 km) in width. The capital city of Providence is located at the head of the bay. A number of islands are located in the bay. The largest are Conanicut, Prudence, and Aquidneck (also called Rhode) Islands. The city of Newport is located on Aquidneck Island.

Three islands in Narragansett Bay — Prudence, Hope, and Patience Islands — are protected by the U.S. government as the Narragansett Bay Estuarine Research Reserve. The reserve, established in 1980, covers more than 2,353 acres (952 ha) of land and 1,591 acres (644 ha) of surrounding water. The reserve is the site of cliffs, salt marshes, creeks, waterfalls, and beaches. Prudence Island is home to the densest population of white-tailed deer in New England.

Average January temperature
Providence: 28°F (-2°C)
Block Island: 31°F (-1°C)

Average July temperature
Providence: 72°F (22°C)
Block Island: 70°F (21°C)

Average yearly rainfall
Providence:
 43 inches (109 cm)
Block Island:
 41 inches (104 cm)

Average yearly snowfall
Providence:
 38 inches (97 cm)
Block Island:
 21 inches (53 cm)

DID YOU KNOW?

Point Judith Light, located at the western entrance to Narragansett Bay, was built in 1857. The light still guides boats past a dangerous section of Rhode Island's coast.

Largest Lakes

Scituate Reservoir
4,563 acres (1,847 hectares)

Worden Pond
1,043 acres (422 ha)

Watchaug Pond
1,000 acres (405 ha)

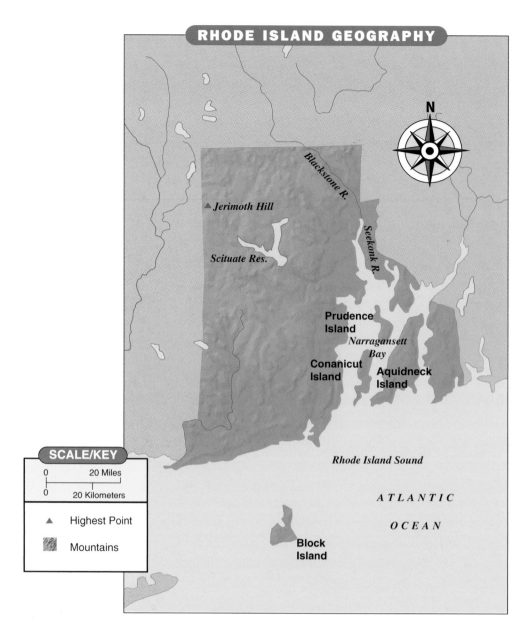

Blackstone R.

▲ *Jerimoth Hill*

Scituate Res.

Seekonk R.

Prudence Island

Narragansett Bay

Conanicut Island

Aquidneck Island

Rhode Island Sound

ATLANTIC

OCEAN

Block Island

SCALE/KEY

0	20 Miles
0	20 Kilometers

▲ Highest Point

Mountains

The New England Upland

The New England Upland occupies the northwestern third of the state. It features steep hills, rocky cliffs, and land that is higher than the rest of the state. The state's highest point, Jerimoth Hill, is here. Many small ponds and lakes are found among the hills. The New England Upland is characterized by rocky, poorly drained soils. Much of the region is forested. It is far less urbanized than the Coastal Lowlands.

Plants and Animals

About 60 percent of Rhode Island is forested. These forests contain more than fifty different types of trees and hundreds of types of plants. Trees that grow in the state include oak, birch, beech, cedar, elm, hickory, pine, and maple. The red maple is Rhode Island's state tree. Wildflowers and plants include daisies, goldenrod, hollies, lilies, mountain laurels, and violets. Some of these plants are listed as endangered and are protected by state and federal law.

Rhode Island's many forested areas are perfect shelters for an array of wild creatures. The largest wild animals found here are white-tailed deer. In recent years, black bears have made their way into the state from other areas. Other smaller animals include raccoon, coyotes, squirrels, mink, woodchucks, red foxes, and opossums. Freshwater ponds and lakes are home to fish, reptiles, and amphibians.

Hundreds of species of birds are also native to Rhode Island. They include gulls, herons, cormorants, terns, and ducks. Further inland, bird-watchers can find red-tailed hawks, ospreys, chickadees, blue jays, wild turkeys, and many other feathered creatures. Forty different endangered or rare bird species can be found on Block Island alone.

The waters off the state's coast abound with a large variety of fish and shellfish, including cod, flounder, halibut, tuna, clams, scallops, oysters, lobsters, and crabs. During the winter, harbor seals can be seen off the islands in Narragansett Bay.

Major Rivers

Blackstone River
48 miles (77 km)

Pawcatuck River
30 miles (48 km)

Pawtuxet River
11 miles (18 km)

▼ Forests and water combine to form habitats for a variety of wildlife throughout Rhode Island. Ducks and Canada geese line the ponds of Roger Williams Park in Providence.

Cradle of the Industrial Revolution

> Outsiders think that we don't care for anything but chasing the dollar but we know better — and say nothing.
>
> — *Tiverton fisherman, quoted as part of the Federal Writers' Project, 1938–1939*

Since Rhode Island was first settled in the 1600s, it has experienced economic highs and lows. Early on, agriculture, shipping, shipbuilding, fishing, and whaling were all important. In 1790, the Rhode Island economy was transformed when Moses Brown and Samuel Slater built the first cotton mill in Pawtucket. That event marked the beginning of the Industrial Revolution in the United States. It also began a golden age for the state's economy. Before long, other factories sprang up throughout the state, and manufacturing supplanted all other industries.

During the Great Depression that began in 1929, Rhode Island suffered hard times and lagged again following World War II. More recently, however, the state has made a comeback. Today, services such as health, insurance, and real estate are a major part of the economy, while manufacturing remains important. Tourism has also grown as more people discover the small state's many treasures, especially its beautiful coastline and many public beaches. Between 1999 and 2000, Rhode Island realized a greater percentage growth in gross state product (GSP) than any other state in the nation. Rhode Island's GSP rose by 10.7 percent, compared with a 4.5 percent increase nationwide.

Top Employers
(of workers age sixteen and over)

Services	44.6%
Manufacturing	16.4%
Wholesale and retail trade	15.5%
Finance, insurance, and real estate	6.9%
Construction	5.4%
Federal, state, and local government (including military)	4.5%
Transportation, communications, and other public utilities	6.2%
Agriculture, forestry, fisheries, and mining	0.5%

Agriculture, Mining, and Fishing

Agriculture, forestry, and mining play a small role in Rhode Island's economy. The state has about seven hundred farms averaging 75 acres (30 ha) in size. More than 80 percent of the state's yearly farm income comes from crop production, with livestock and related products accounting for the rest.

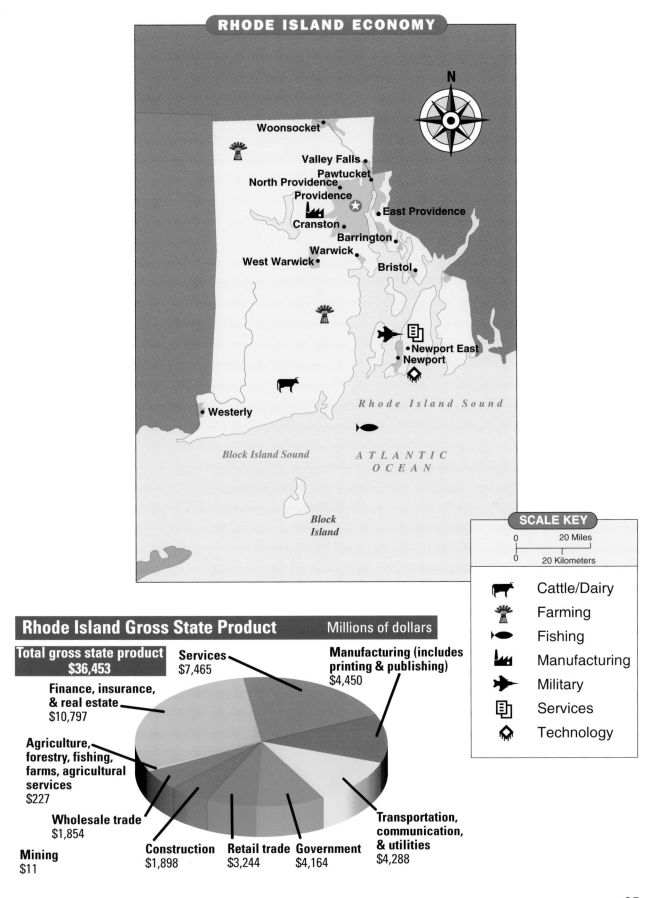

RHODE ISLAND ECONOMY

Woonsocket

Valley Falls
Pawtucket
North Providence
Providence
East Providence
Cranston
Barrington
Warwick
West Warwick
Bristol

Newport East
Newport

Rhode Island Sound

Westerly

Block Island Sound

ATLANTIC OCEAN

Block Island

SCALE KEY

| 0 | 20 Miles |
| 0 | 20 Kilometers |

- Cattle/Dairy
- Farming
- Fishing
- Manufacturing
- Military
- Services
- Technology

Rhode Island Gross State Product — Millions of dollars

Total gross state product $36,453

- Services $7,465
- Manufacturing (includes printing & publishing) $4,450
- Finance, insurance, & real estate $10,797
- Agriculture, forestry, fishing, farms, agricultural services $227
- Wholesale trade $1,854
- Mining $11
- Construction $1,898
- Retail trade $3,244
- Government $4,164
- Transportation, communication, & utilities $4,288

Greenhouse and nursery products are the most valuable of the state's farm products. Another important product is milk. Most of the state's mining income comes from limestone, granite, crushed stone, and gravel. Some gemstones, however, are also produced.

Rhode Island has a significant fishing industry. Each year, fishing adds about $79 million to the state's coffers. The main fish taken by Rhode Island fishing boats include flounder, lobsters, clams, squid, and scallops.

Manufacturing

In 2000, manufacturing accounted for about 12 percent of Rhode Island's GSP. Manufacturing remains centered around the capital city of Providence. The most important manufactured goods that come out of the state include fabricated metals, precision instruments, and clothing and textiles. Other products that are made in Rhode Island include jewelry, toys, electronic goods, industrial machinery, transportation equipment, and processed goods.

One well-known manufacturing company in Rhode Island is Electric Boat, a subsidiary of General Dynamics. This company makes nuclear-powered attack submarines for the U.S. Navy. Its plant in North Kingstown has been in operation since 1973. The steel hulls of the submarines are made here. About 9,800 people work for Electric Boat in Rhode Island.

Health, Tourism, and Other Services

Services are the number one industry in Rhode Island. Services that contribute to the state's economic welfare include health, insurance, real estate, and tourism. In 1998, health services were the number-one service industry in the state. The state is home to fourteen medical hospitals and two psychiatric hospitals. Major medical centers in Rhode Island include Lifespan, St. Joseph, and Roger Williams hospitals.

▲ Rhode Island's beaches attract thousands of tourists each year.

Jewelry Capital of the World

Providence has laid claim to the title of "jewelry capital of the world" since the eighteenth century. In 1794, goldsmith and watch repairer Nehemiah Dodge invented a way to coat a cheaper metal with a thin layer of gold. Soon, all fashionable Rhode Island ladies were wearing Dodge's gold-plated baubles and bangles. Dodge's business prospered, and apprentices flocked to the area to learn the jewelry-making trade. By 1805, thirty artisans were working in Providence making jewelry. Today, more than thirty-five thousand people are employed by one thousand Providence jewelry manufacturers. Rhode Island companies produce jewelry, military pins and badges, key chains, medals, and other metal fashion items.

Other important service industries in the state include those for business, educational, and social services.

Tourism is an industry that is becoming more important to Rhode Island. Every year, about fifteen million tourists visit the state. Rhode Island's sandy beaches and water activities are the biggest draw. More than forty of these beautiful beaches are open to the public. The small state has many historic sites as well, with twelve state parks to entertain guests. Block Island is also an important vacation destination.

▲ The battleship USS *Iowa* is guided into Narragansett Bay. The *Iowa* joins the aircraft carriers USS *Saratoga* and USS *Forrestal,* which are docked at the Naval Education and Training Center in Newport.

Government

The presence of the U.S. Navy in Rhode Island dates back to the Civil War, when the Naval Academy was moved out of Annapolis, Maryland, to the safety of Newport. Today, the navy operates the Naval Education and Training Center, Naval Undersea Warfare Center, and Naval War College in the city. These three facilities provide training and advanced combat technology for the nation's maritime military force. More than seven thousand military and civilian personnel are employed here, and more than two thousand students attend training sessions each day.

Transportation

Rhode Island has an excellent transportation system. The state has about 6,110 miles (9,831 km) of roads, including a major interstate that cuts through the state from Connecticut to Massachusetts. Providence has an excellent public transportation system, and train services connect the city to Boston and other major metropolitan areas throughout the region. Theodore Francis (T. F.) Green Airport, located in Warwick, continues to grow in size and serve larger numbers of passengers each year. The airport was named for a famous Providence-born politician who served the state for many years as governor and U.S. senator.

Made in Rhode Island

Leading farm products and crops
Greenhouse and nursery products
Milk
Eggs
Potatoes
Hay

Other products
Costume jewelry
Toys
Machinery
Fabricated metals
Precision instruments
Clothing and textiles
Electronics
Printed materials
Rubber and plastic items

Major Airports		
Airport	Location	Passengers per year (2000)
Theodore Francis (T. F.) Green	Warwick	5,430,938

Rhode Island's Government

> Rare felicity of the times when it is permitted to think what you like and say what you think.
>
> *— Inscription on Rhode Island's State House dome, from* Histories *by the Roman historian Tacitus, A.D. 109*

For more than 175 years, Rhode Island governed itself using the Royal Charter granted to the colony by King Charles II in 1663. In 1842, a more liberal constitution was enacted by state lawmakers and ratified the next year. Since then, the constitution has undergone a series of changes, called amendments. A constitutional amendment can be proposed by the state's legislature or a constitutional convention. Then the proposed amendment must be approved by a majority of voters during the next general election.

The system of government in Rhode Island — just like that of the U.S. federal government — is divided into three branches: executive, legislative, and judicial. The executive branch administers laws, the legislative branch makes laws, and the judicial branch interprets laws.

The Executive Branch

The governor of Rhode Island is the state's chief executive. The governor makes sure that state laws are carried out effectively and directs how money shall be collected and spent in the state. One of the governor's most important jobs is to appoint capable people to government offices. The governor appoints judges for the courts, members of commissions and boards, and people to fill vacancies in government offices. The state senate usually has to approve the governor's appointments.

Another important power held by the governor is the right to veto proposed legislation. The legislature can override the governor's veto by a three-fifths majority vote of members present in both houses. The governor's other

State Constitution

"**We**, the people of the State of Rhode Island and Providence Plantations, grateful to Almighty God for the civil and religious liberty which He hath so long permitted us to enjoy, and looking to Him for a blessing upon our endeavors to secure and to transmit the same, unimpaired, to succeeding generations, do ordain and establish this Constitution of government."

— Preamble to the 1842 Rhode Island State Constitution

Elected Posts in the Executive Branch		
Office	Length of Term	Term Limits
Governor	4 years	2 consecutive terms
Lieutenant Governor	4 years	2 consecutive terms
Secretary of State	4 years	2 consecutive terms
Attorney General	4 years	2 consecutive terms
General Treasurer	4 years	2 consecutive terms

duties include commanding the state's military and naval forces, convening special sessions of the legislature, and granting pardons or reprieves to convicted criminals.

In addition to the governor, there are four other elected posts in the executive branch. One of these positions is that of lieutenant governor. The lieutenant governor assists the governor and presides over the state senate. If the governor should become unfit or incapable of doing the job, the lieutenant governor would take over.

The Legislative Branch

The Rhode Island state legislature is called the General Assembly. It is composed of a senate with fifty members and a house of representatives with one hundred members. The General Assembly's most important job is to write and pass new state laws. The General Assembly meets annually in Providence, beginning every year on the first Tuesday of January and continuing for at least sixty days or until its work is complete. That is the regular session, but special sessions can also be called by the governor.

▼ Construction of the Rhode Island State House in Providence began in 1895. It features the fourth-largest freestanding dome in the world.

The Judicial Branch

The judicial branch consists of judges presiding over courts, with each court subject to review by a higher court. Rhode Island's judicial

system consists of six courts. The state supreme court is the highest in Rhode Island. It makes the final decision in all cases except those where state law conflicts with federal law. The five supreme court justices are appointed by the governor, with the General Assembly's approval. The justices may keep their appointment "during good behavior." This means that they can serve for as long as they perform their jobs capably. On Rhode Island's supreme court, one judge is selected as chief justice. The other four are known as associate justices.

The superior court is the state's second highest court. The twenty-two justices of the superior court are appointed by the governor with the approval of the state senate. Below the superior court is the district court. The five divisions of this court function as the state's chief trial courts. The thirteen district court judges are also appointed by the governor with the approval of the senate. Other courts include family court, workers' compensation court, and traffic tribunal. The governor, with the senate's approval, also appoints these judges. In addition, cities and towns may have municipal and probate courts.

Local Government

Government is also divided in another way: federal, state, and local. While the federal government of the United States has powers over the whole nation, state governments such as Rhode Island's have powers over their own state matters. Within the states, too, there are local governments with powers over special local matters.

Although the state is divided into five counties, these counties are judicial districts and have no government structure. The main units of local government are Rhode Island's thirty-nine municipalities, or cities and towns. Many of the municipalities elect a mayor and/or a council to run the local government. Others use a manager or administrator to make sure their government runs smoothly and effectively. Each municipality controls its

General Assembly			
House	Number of Members	Length of Term	Term Limits
Senate	50 senators	2 years	None
House of Representatives	100 representatives	2 years	None

education system, land, and zoning. Most municipal funds come from a property tax.

National Representation

Like all states, Rhode Island has two senators in the U.S. Senate. Because of the state's small population, it has just two representatives in the U.S. House of Representatives. In 2004, Rhode Island will retain four Electoral College votes, the same as in recent elections.

Rhode Island Politics

Until 1933, Rhode Island's governors were most often Republican. From the mid-1930s to 1985, Democrats usually held power in the governor's office and the General Assembly. Since 1985, voters have elected two Republican govenors and one Democratic governor but left the Democrats in power in the legislature.

In 2002, one of the state's U.S. senators was a Republican; the other senator and both U.S. congressmen were Democrats. During the 2000 presidential election, a greater percentage of voters backed Democratic nominee Al Gore than in any other state.

▼ Members of the Rhode Island state senate meet to consider legislation.

The Independent Man

High atop Rhode Island's State House stands a giant gold-covered bronze statue of a man. Known as Independent Man, the statue has towered 278 feet (85 m) over Providence since December 18, 1899, when the capitol building was completed. Independent Man is 11 feet (3 m) tall and weighs more than 500 pounds (227 kilograms). He carries a 14-foot (4-m) spear, and an anchor lies at his feet. The statue symbolizes the independent spirit of state founder Roger Williams and Rhode Islanders past and present. Sculpted by George Brewster, Independent Man has braved plenty of wild weather, including blizzards, hurricanes, and twenty-seven lightning strikes. The statue was taken off the dome and repaired in 1975.

A Wealth of Things to Do

> The Elms to be appreciated must be seen and not less than three hundred ladies were present during the reception at which Mr. and Mrs. Berwind received.
>
> — *A news clip about the Elms, a Newport mansion, from the* Newport Herald, *1901*

Visitors to Rhode Island may be surprised by the wide variety of activities that can be enjoyed throughout the state. For history buffs, there are plenty of state parks and historic sites where they can learn all about Rhode Island's founding and development over the years. People looking for a spot to pass a rainy day will find libraries and museums. Arts-oriented visitors have a wide array of cultural activities from which to choose. Tourists can also enjoy plenty of sand, sun, and surf. Even wine lovers will love it here: Rhode Island is home to four vineyards and wineries. This little state has something for everyone!

Historic Sites

Rhode Island is home to many sites and attractions that take travelers back to another time. The state has a number of historic homes, from the earliest colonial period to the twentieth century. One of the oldest is the Clemence-Irons House in Johnston, built around 1680. This house is a unique structure known as a stone-ender, a building framed in wood with end walls made from stone. Stone-enders were popular during colonial times. People interested in the Revolutionary War period can tour the Gilbert Stuart

DID YOU KNOW?

Watch Hill in Westerly is home to the Flying Horse Carousel, considered the oldest in the nation. It may have been built as early as 1867. Carousel horses hang from chains attached overhead. The faster the carousel goes, the farther out horse and rider swing.

▼ George Washington sits for the portrait by Gilbert Stuart that appears on the one dollar bill.

Birthplace in Saunderstown, home of the artist who painted George Washington's portrait for the $1 bill. Visitors can also tour the Homestead in Coventry, home to Nathanael Greene, Washington's second-in-command during the war. There are also a number of forts, including Butts Hill Fort in Portsmouth, the site of the only Revolutionary War land battle in the state, the Battle of Rhode Island. On August 29, 1778, the Black Regiment of Rhode Island bravely defended Portsmouth against the British.

In Newport, tourists can relive Rhode Island's Gilded Age by visiting the huge mansions that overlook the Atlantic Ocean. During the late 1800s, "summer cottages" such as Rosecliff, Beechwood, the Breakers, and Marble House were built by the richest families in the United States. Many of these grand homes still contain the ornate furnishings and works of art that made them famous throughout the world. Several of the mansions are National Historic Landmarks, lasting symbols of a bygone era.

While in Newport, history buffs can also visit Touro Synagogue, the oldest Jewish place of worship in the United States. Built in 1763, the synagogue served as a meeting place for the Rhode Island General Assembly from 1781 to 1784. In 1781, a town meeting was held there when George Washington visited Newport. Other famous Newport sites include the White Horse Inn, one of the oldest U.S. taverns.

Hammersmith Farm

One of many beautiful homes in Newport is Hammersmith Farm. Built in 1887, the twenty-eight-room house was later owned by Hugh Auchincloss, stepfather of Jacqueline Bouvier. As a teenager, she spent many summers at Hammersmith Farm. In 1953, she married John F. Kennedy, a bright and promising senator from Massachusetts. The couple's wedding reception was held at Hammersmith Farm. After Kennedy was elected U.S. president, he and Jackie used the big home as a summer White House from 1961 to 1963. Hammersmith Farm is now open to the public.

Green Animals Topiary Garden, in Portsmouth, is one of the nation's largest and oldest gardens of topiary — the art of cutting or trimming trees and shrubs into ornamental shapes.

Libraries and Museums

Rhode Island's first library, the Redwood Library and Athenaeum in Newport, opened in 1750. The library is the oldest lending library in the United States. Rhode Island's first free public library was established in Woonsocket in 1856. Today, the state has many valuable public and research libraries, including the Providence Public Library and the Brown University libraries. State and federal publications and documents are stored in the State House at the State Library, which is open to the public.

Rhode Island has a number of important museums. In Providence, kids will love the Providence Children's Museum, where they can climb a tree, explore a cave, build a fountain, and tour a mini animal hospital. The Rhode Island School of Design Museum traces the history of art from ancient times to the present. A must-see museum in Bristol is the Haffenreffer Museum of Anthropology, home

▲ Some of Rhode Island's lighthouses are now museums that display artifacts of the state's nautical heritage.

to an extensive collection of treasures from Rhode Island, North America, and other parts of the world.

Like Providence, Newport has a wealth of museums. One point of interest is the Artillery Company of Newport's museum, filled with weapons, uniforms, and other relics from U.S. military history. Other Newport museums include the Doll Museum, Museum of Yachting, National Museum of American Illustration, and the Thames Science Center.

Communications

More than thirty newspapers are published in Rhode Island. Most are published only once a week, but six are published every day. The leading dailies include the *Providence Journal-Bulletin, Pawtucket Times,* and *Newport Daily News.* The first newspaper in Rhode Island was the *Rhode Island Gazette,* published in Newport in 1732 by James Franklin, the brother of Benjamin Franklin. The state is also served by five television stations and twenty-six radio stations.

Music and Theater

Rhode Island is home to a wealth of cultural opportunities. Broadway shows, world-renowned entertainers, and

▼ The Australian dance troupe Tap Dogs perform outside the Providence Performing Arts Center.

▶ Performers at Newport's JVC Jazz Festival. Each year, the festival draws thousands of visitors from around the nation.

children's programs can all be seen on the stage of the Providence Performing Arts Center. The oldest arts auditorium in the state is the Veterans Memorial Auditorium Arts and Cultural Center in Providence, founded in 1928. Concerts, plays, and other events attract audiences to the center from around the area. The center is also the home of the Rhode Island Philharmonic Orchestra. The Trinity Repertory Company, founded in Providence in 1964, is a well-known theatrical group. The group has made four television productions and toured internationally. A well-known annual music event is the JVC Jazz Festival, held in Newport. Some of jazz's greatest artists have appeared at the festival since its beginnings in 1954. Rhode Island has had its fair share of famous musicians, too. George M. Cohan, an actor and singer who wrote successful Broadway musicals in the early 1900s, hailed from Providence, as did singer and actor Nelson Eddy. Bobby Hackett, a famous trumpet player who played with Cab Calloway, Benny Goodman, Glenn Miller, and Louis Armstrong, was also born in Rhode Island's capital city.

Sports

Rhode Island is a great place to spot sports stars of the future. That's because a number of professional minor league teams call the state home. The Providence Bruins are an American Hockey League (AHL) team. They are the farm team of the Boston Bruins of the National Hockey League (NHL). The Pawtucket Red Sox, an AAA

International League team, is the farm team of major league baseball's Boston Red Sox. Soccer fans can check out the Rhode Island Stingrays, a United Soccer League team based in East Providence. For sports fans who must have major league excitement, the New England Patriots of the National Football League (NFL) have held their training camp at Bryant College in Smithfield each summer for more than twenty-five years.

Tennis in the United States got its start in Rhode Island. The game was a favorite of Newport's rich and famous during the Gilded Age. In 1881, the first U.S. National Championship was held in Newport. Visitors to the city can see the oldest grass courts in the nation at the International Tennis Hall of Fame, which celebrates the history of professional tennis in the United States. Tennis greats who have been inducted into the Hall of Fame include Arthur Ashe, Jimmy Connors, Chris Evert, John McEnroe, and Martina Navratilova.

Known as the "sailing capital of America," Newport is also famous for yachting. From 1930 to 1983, the prestigious America's Cup race was held off the coast of Newport. The race had its start in 1851, when yachtsman George L. Schuyler encouraged competition between foreign nations by donating a "challenge cup." Although the race is no longer held in Newport, people can visit the America's Cup Hall of Fame. This exhibit at the Herreshoff Marine Museum chronicles the long history of the race.

▶ The original of this photo of Lizzie Murphy resides at the Baseball Hall of Fame in Cooperstown, New York.

Rhode Island Greats

Napoleon "Nap" Lajoie was an outstanding baseball player who became the American League's first batting champion. Born in Woonsocket in 1874, Lajoie played second base for three major league teams from 1896 to 1916. In 1901, Lajoie batted .422, an American League record that still stands today. In 1937, Lajoie was inducted into the Baseball Hall of Fame.

Known as "Spike" to her teammates, Lizzie Murphy was better known to fans as the "Queen of Baseball." Born in Warren in 1894, Murphy began playing amateur ball at the age of fifteen. In 1918, she was signed by the semiprofessional Boston All-Stars to play first base. In 1922, she was chosen to play on the American League's All-Star team during a charity game against the Boston Red Sox, making her the first woman to play in the major leagues.

Renowned Rhode Islanders

We fight, get beat, rise, and fight again.
— *Nathanael Greene, Revolutionary War general, 1781*

Following are only a few of the thousands of people who were born, died, or spent much of their lives in Rhode Island and made extraordinary contributions to the state and the nation.

ANNE HUTCHINSON
RELIGIOUS LEADER

BORN: *June or July 1591, Alford, England*
DIED: *August or September 1643, New York, NY*

In 1634, Anne Marbury Hutchinson, her husband, and fourteen children moved from England to Boston, Massachusetts. Hutchinson became active as a religious leader in the colony, attracting a number of followers, many of them women. But in a time when women were meant to be seen and not heard, her views also attracted negative attention — especially when she encouraged others to rebel against Puritan views. After just three years in the colony, Hutchinson was brought to trial for criticizing the Puritans, was found guilty and banished from Massachusetts. Hutchinson and some of her followers moved to Rhode Island in 1638, where they founded the town of Portsmouth. This religious freedom fighter remained active in Rhode Island until moving to New York. There, Hutchinson and five of her children were killed by Native Americans.

ANN SMITH FRANKLIN
PUBLISHER

BORN: *October 2, 1696, Boston, MA*
DIED: *April 16, 1763, Newport*

Ann Smith Franklin got into the publishing business by marrying James Franklin, a well-known printer and older brother of Benjamin Franklin. In 1732, James and Ann founded the weekly *Rhode Island Gazette*, the colony's first newspaper. After her husband's death in 1735, Franklin took control of the family printing business — and James's title of colony printer. With the help of her three children, the Widow Franklin, as she was known, wrote and published almanacs as well as the *Newport Mercury* newspaper. She also obtained permission to print paper money and such legal documents as ballots, mortgages, and ships' registrations for the colony of Rhode Island.

ESEK HOPKINS
NAVY COMMANDER

BORN: *April 26, 1718, Scituate*
DIED: *February 26, 1802, Providence*

Esek Hopkins grew up on a farm but became a sailor as a young man. He eventually became commander of a fleet of merchant ships. During the French and Indian War, he was a privateer, a sailor paid by the government to capture and plunder enemy ships. In 1775, Hopkins was appointed the first commander in chief of the newly formed Continental Navy. Commodore Hopkins had the difficult task of pulling the navy together and securing enough men and supplies to make it a success. In 1778, Congress dismissed him for not acting quickly enough.

NATHANAEL GREENE
PATRIOT

BORN: *August 7, 1742, Warwick*
DIED: *June 19, 1786, Savannah, GA*

Nathanael Greene was one of many Rhode Islanders willing to lay down his

life for independence during the Revolutionary War. In 1775, Greene was given command of Rhode Island's forces and ordered to march to Boston to battle the British. Greene's bravery and valor impressed General George Washington, who made the Rhode Islander a major general. During the early years of the war, Greene fought in the battles of Trenton, Princeton, Brandywine, and Germantown. In 1780, he was given command of the southern revolutionary army, a post second only to General Washington. Greene succeeded in weakening British forces in the region. After the war, he retired to Georgia. He died of sunstroke at the age of forty-three.

GILBERT STUART
ARTIST

BORN: *December 3, 1755, North Kingston*
DIED: *July 9, 1828, Boston, MA*

Gilbert Charles Stuart grew up in Newport, sketching landscapes, animals, and people he met there. At the age of nineteen, Stuart moved to London to study with American painter Benjamin West. When he returned to the United States, he quickly earned a reputation as the top portrait painter of his day. During his career, Stuart became known as the "father of American portraiture," creating more than a thousand portraits. Stuart's sitters included John Adams, Thomas Jefferson, and James Madison. He also painted three famous pictures of George Washington, one of which appears on the $1 bill. Today, Stuart's work is seen in important art museums across the country, including the National Gallery of Art in Washington, D.C.

AMBROSE BURNSIDE
CIVIL WAR GENERAL

BORN: *May 23, 1824, Liberty, IN*
DIED: *September 13, 1881, Bristol*

During the Civil War, General Ambrose Everett Burnside — a West Point graduate who settled in Rhode Island in the 1850s — led the First Regiment of Rhode Island Detached Militia at the battles of Bull Run and Antietam. After Antietam, he was leader of the Army of the Potomac for a short time. He was elected governor of Rhode Island and a U.S. senator after the war. His distinctive facial hair led to a phrase that survives today: sideburns.

EDWARD BANNISTER
ARTIST

BORN: *November 1828, St. Andrews, New Brunswick, Canada*
DIED: *January 9, 1901, Providence*

One of the most prominent landscape painters of his time, African-American artist Edward Mitchell Bannister began painting watercolors at the age of ten in the port town of St. Andrews, New Brunswick. As a young man, Bannister moved to Boston and, while working as a barber, learned the new art of photography. He continued to paint,

creating landscapes, seascapes, and realistic portraits of black life in America. In 1870, the artist moved to Providence. Here, his work attracted attention, and many wealthy patrons bought his paintings to display in their homes. In 1876, Bannister was the first African-American artist to win a national award for his work.

IDA LEWIS
LIGHTHOUSE KEEPER

BORN: *February 25, 1842, Newport*
DIED: *October 24, 1911, Newport*

The daughter of a lighthouse keeper near Newport, Idawalley Zorada Lewis took over her father's duties after he had a stroke. For the next fifty years, Lewis tended the Lime Rock Lighthouse, rescuing a number of sailors. Her first rescue was in 1858, when she saved four men whose boat had capsized. In 1869, one of her rescues was reported in a New York newspaper, and she became famous across the nation. Susan B. Anthony, the famed women's rights leader, used Lewis as an example of a competent woman. In later years, Lewis was awarded a Gold Lifesaving Medal by the U.S. Life-Saving Service and a lifetime pension by the Carnegie Hero Fund.

MATILDA SISSIERETTA JONES
OPERA SINGER

BORN: *January 5, 1869, Portsmouth, VA*
DIED: *June 24, 1933, Providence*

Matilda Sissieretta Joyner Jones used her powerful soprano voice to break color barriers in the United States. A well-known concert singer in the late 1800s, Jones first studied music at the Providence Academy of Music. She later became the first African-American woman to perform at Carnegie Hall in New York. During her career, "Madame Jones" performed in Madison Square Garden and at the White House for President Benjamin Harrison. Although she was considered for a singing role at the Metropolitan Opera, she was turned away because of her race. From 1895 to 1916, Jones and a group of musicians toured the world. Afterward, she retired to Providence.

GEORGE M. COHAN
ENTERTAINER

BORN: *July 3, 1878, Providence*
DIED: *November 5, 1942, New York, NY*

George Michael Cohan was an all-American actor, writer, and producer who had show business in his blood. Cohan grew up in a vaudeville family and first performed on stage at age nine. He presented his first show on Broadway in 1901. In 1904, he appeared onstage as Yankee Doodle Boy, a role that became forever associated with him. Cohan was most popular during the 1920s, when his Broadway shows played to packed audiences. Some of the most famous of the many songs he wrote were "I'm a Yankee Doodle Dandy," "You're a Grand Old Flag," and "Give My Regards to Broadway." In 1942, Cohan was awarded the Congressional Medal of Honor for his World War I song "Over There." The same year, an award-winning film about his life, *Yankee Doodle Dandy*, was released.

H. P. LOVECRAFT
AUTHOR

BORN: *August 20, 1890, Providence*
DIED: *March 15, 1937, Providence*

Howard Phillips Lovecraft was a writer of science fiction and horror stories. A sickly child, Lovecraft spent much of his youth reading spooky stories by Edgar Allan Poe and other writers. Soon, he began writing his own terror-filled tales. Some of Lovecraft's first successes came in the pulp-fiction magazine *Weird Tales*. Later, some of these stories were collected and published together in books. During his lifetime, Lovecraft struggled to earn a living writing, and he died in poverty. Many modern horror writers have read and admired Lovecraft, including Ray Bradbury, Stephen King, and Peter Straub.

CHRIS VAN ALLSBURG
AUTHOR AND ILLUSTRATOR

BORN: *June 18, 1949, Grand Rapids, MI*

Chris Van Allsburg is an award-winning author and illustrator of children's books. In 1972, Van Allsburg moved to Providence to attend the Rhode Island School of Design (RISD). After receiving a master's degree in sculpture, he remained to teach at RISD. He published his first book, *The Garden of Abdul Gasazi,* in 1979. Since then, Van Allsburg has created some of the most popular children's fiction ever, including the Caldecott Medal-winning books *Jumanji* and *The Polar Express*. The award of the Caldecott Medal to Van Allsburg recognizes his gift for telling stories through art. In 1995, *Jumanji* was made into a movie starring Robin Williams.

Rhode Island

History At-A-Glance

1524
Giovanni da Verrazano visits the Rhode Island area.

1614
Adriaen Block explores the coast of Rhode Island and names Block Island.

1636
Roger Williams founds Providence, the first permanent white settlement in Rhode Island.

1638
Anne Hutchinson, exiled from the Massachusetts Bay Colony, founds Portsmouth.

1663
Charles II of Great Britain grants a royal charter to the state of Rhode Island and Providence Plantations.

1675
Colonists defeat local Native Americans in King Philip's War to take control of the area.

1772
Rhode Island patriots burn the *Gaspee*, a British customs ship.

1776
Rhode Island is the first colony to renounce allegiance to King George III of Great Britain.

1776–79
British troops occupy Newport, burning many buildings and causing resident patriots to flee.

1790
Rhode Island is the last of the thirteen original colonies to ratify the U.S. Constitution.

1790
Moses Brown and Samuel Slater begin the U.S. Industrial Revolution when they open a cotton mill in Pawtucket.

1828
The state sets up and subsidizes a public school system.

1600   **1700**   **1800**

1492
Christopher Columbus comes to New World.

1607
Capt. John Smith and three ships land on Virginia coast and start first English settlement in New World — Jamestown.

1754–63
French and Indian War.

1773
Boston Tea Party.

1776
Declaration of Independence adopted July 4.

1777
Articles of Confederation adopted by Continental Congress.

1787
U.S. Constitution written.

1812–14
War of 1812.

United States

History At-A-Glance

1842
Dorr's Rebellion spurs lawmakers to liberalize the state's constitution.

1868
Rhode Island enters a Gilded Age of economic prosperity. Thousands of immigrants from around the world flood into the state to work at factory and other jobs.

1869
Rose Island Lighthouse, located on an island off Newport, is built.

1888
Marble House, the palatial "summer cottage" of the William Vanderbilts, is completed in Newport.

1897
Rhode Island adopts a state flag that bears a golden anchor and the motto "Hope."

1910
The United States Census tallies Rhode Island's population at more than 540,000.

1929
The Great Depression hits Rhode Island hard, causing factories to close and throwing thousands of state residents out of work.

1931
Hillsgrove State Airport, the first state-owned airport, opens. It is later renamed Theodore Francis (T. F.) Green Airport.

1930–83
The America's Cup, the most important challenge in yachting, is held in Newport.

1954
Hurricane Carol wreaks havoc across the state, causing millions of dollars in damage.

1996
Rhode Island adopts a new state song, "Rhode Island's It for Me."

1990s–2000
Rhode Island and its capital city, Providence, experience a renaissance as the economy booms.

1800   **1900**   **2000**

1848
Gold discovered in California draws eighty thousand prospectors in the 1849 Gold Rush.

1861–65
Civil War.

1869
Transcontinental railroad completed.

1917–18
U.S. involvement in World War I.

1929
Stock market crash ushers in Great Depression.

1941–45
U.S. involvement in World War II.

1950–53
U.S. fights in the Korean War.

1964–73
U.S. involvement in Vietnam War.

2000
George W. Bush wins the closest presidential election in history.

2001
A terrorist attack in which four hijacked airliners crash into New York City's World Trade Center, the Pentagon, and farmland in western Pennsylvania leaves thousands dead or injured.

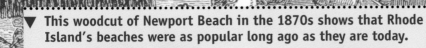
▼ This woodcut of Newport Beach in the 1870s shows that Rhode Island's beaches were as popular long ago as they are today.

Festivals and Fun for All

Check web site for exact date and directions.

Blessing of the Fleet, Narragansett

Boats of all types are blessed by local clergy at this annual festival. The weekend-long event also features a road race, seafood festival, and boat decorating competition.
www.narragansettri.com/lions/index.htm

Festival of Lights, North Kingstown

For one weekend each winter, thousands of white lights combine to transform historic Wickford Village into a wonderland.
www.northkingstown.com/new_events_template_1.html

Gaspee Days, Warwick

This annual celebration includes a mock colonial battle, a colonial costume contest, a parade — and a re-creation of the burning of the British ship *Gaspee*.
www.gaspee.com

Harvest Fair, Middletown

This old-fashioned fall fair, complete with games, hay and pony rides, crafts, and food, is held annually at the Norman Bird Sanctuary.
www.normanbirdsanctuary.org

Jack O' Lantern Spectacular, Providence

In October, more than five thousand carved pumpkins light up a 3-acre (1.2 ha) wooded trail through the Roger Williams Park Zoo.
www.rwpzoo.org/jackolantern/code/spectacular.html

JVC Jazz Festival, Newport

This weekend-long outdoor celebration of jazz and blues music takes place in Fort Adams State Park.
www.festivalproductions.net

Newport International Film Festival, Newport

Each year, movie fans can check out the latest foreign and U.S. films at this weeklong festival.
www.newportfilmfestival.com

Newport International Polo Series, Newport

Horses and riders from around the world compete in Newport throughout the summer.
www.newportinternationalpolo.com

Newport Winter Festival, Newport

For those who'd rather celebrate than hibernate, New England's largest winter extravaganza includes more than 150 events to commemorate the snowy season.
www.newportevents.com

Ocean State Marathon, Providence

The marathon is an annual 26.2-mile (42.2 km) road race for runners through the state's capital.
www.osm26.com

Pawcatuck River Duck Race, Westerly

Thousands of bright yellow rubber duckies race down the river for fun and prizes.
www.westerlychamber.org

Pet Walk, Providence

Proud of your pets? Take them to this annual promenade for pets at Roger Williams Park, sponsored by the Providence Animal Rescue League. They might even win a prize!
www.parl.org

Pokanoket Wampanoag Federation Powwow, Pawtucket

Native American tribes from around the nation get together to dance and celebrate Native culture.
www.geocities.com/pokanoket_tribe

Rhode Island Spring Flower and Garden Show, Providence

About thirty different gardens are on display during this annual weekend-long event.
www.flowershow.com

▶ Spectators often line the banks of the Providence River to watch the Waterfire bonfires. The fires are suspended on floats above the river and tended by black-clad performers who keep them going from sunset to midnight.

Schweppes Great Chowder Cook-Off, Newport

The creations of more than thirty chefs from around the United States compete annually for the coveted titles of Best Clam Chowder, Best Seafood Chowder, Most Creative Chowder, and Best Clam Cakes.
www.newportfestivals.com

Storytelling Festival, statewide

This annual event, which takes place in different locations around the state, features fascinating fables for the whole family.
www.ristic.org

WaterFire, Providence

Spectacular displays of nearly one hundred bonfires on three Providence rivers take place throughout the year.
www.waterfire.com

Youth Playwriting Competition and Festival, East Providence

Each year, high school students get the chance to submit their original one-act plays. The winners receive prizes and have their plays produced by the All Children's Theatre.
www.actinri.org

Books

Avi. *Finding Providence: The Story of Roger Williams*. New York: HarperCollins, 1997. This book describes the life of Roger Williams and how he came to found Rhode Island.

Fisher, Leonard Everett. *To Bigotry No Sanction: The Story of the Oldest Synagogue in America*. New York: Holiday House, 1999. Learn more about the history of Newport's Touro Synagogue.

Fradin, Dennis B. *The Rhode Island Colony*. Chicago: Children's Press, 1989. Trace the early days of Rhode Island from exploration to statehood.

Lisle, Janet Taylor. *The Art of Keeping Cool*. New York: Atheneum Books for Young Readers, 2000. This award-winning historical fiction novel features a boy who learns about life, death, and prejudice during World War II.

Macaulay, David. *Mill*. Boston: Houghton Mifflin, 1989. Pen-and-ink illustrations take readers into an imaginary New England textile mill during the 1800s.

Web Sites

▶ Official state web site
www.state.ri.us

▶ City of Providence homepage
www.providenceri.com

▶ The Rhode Island Historical Society
www.rihs.org

▶ Rhode Island's official tourism page
www.visitrhodeisland.com

Films and Documentaries

Jones, Dan. *Newport and the Rhode Island Coast*. SITE Productions, 1992. Explore the state's celebrated coastline in this forty-minute video.

Robertson, Tom, and Maria Lane. *America's Castles: Newport Mansions*. A&E Home Video, 1996. Take a tour through the "summer cottages" of America's Gilded Age millionaires.

Youngdahl, Kate. *Roger Williams and Rhode Island*. Schlessinger Media, 1999. The founding of Rhode Island is reenacted at actual historic locations in this short video.